IN THE PARK

IN THE PARK
An Excursion in Four Languages

by ESTHER HAUTZIG
Pictures by EZRA JACK KEATS

THE MACMILLAN COMPANY, NEW YORK
COLLIER-MACMILLAN LIMITED, LONDON

The Macmillan Company, New York
Collier-Macmillan Canada, Ltd., Toronto, Ontario

Library of Congress catalog card number: 68-10067

Printed in the United States of America

FIRST PRINTING

Phonetics checked by the editorial staff of Berlitz Publications, Inc.

For our David
who loves all parks

On a sunny day
Everyone goes to the park
In New York   or Paris,

Moscow

or Madrid.

It is nice in the park. So much
to see and do. Such fun to visit.
In New York   or Paris,

trees   squirrels

arbres   **écureuils**
ahrbr   eh-kew-<u>roy</u>

деревья   **белки**
d'yeh-r'yeh-v'yah   b'<u>yehl</u>-kee

árboles   **ardillas**
<u>ahr</u>-boh-lehs   ahr-<u>dee</u>-l'yahs

Moscow

grass

herbe
ehrb

трава
trah-vah

hierba
yehr-bah

or Madrid
A park has . . .

lampposts

réverbères
reh-vehr-behr

фонарные столбы
fah-nahr-nee-yeh stohl-bee

postes de la luz
pohs-tehs deh lah looth

rocks

rocs
rohk

скалы
skah-lee

rocas
roh-kahs

benches

bancs
bahng

скамьи
sk'ahm-yee

bancos
bahn-kohs

flowers

fleurs
fluhr

цветы
tsv'yeh-<u>tee</u>

flores
<u>floh</u>-rehs

playgrounds

cours de récréation
koor duh reh-kreh-ah-s'yohng

площадки для игры
plah-sh'<u>chahd</u>-kee dl'ya ee-<u>gree</u>

patios de recreo
<u>pah</u>-tee-ohs deh reh-<u>kreh</u>-oh

monuments

monuments
moh-new-mahng

ПАМЯТНИКИ
pah-m'yaht-nee-kee

monumentos
moh-noo-mehn-tohs

pigeons

pigeons
pee-<u>zhohng</u>

голуби
<u>goh</u>-loo-bee

palomas
pah-<u>loh</u>-mahs

fountains

fontaines
fohn-<u>tehn</u>

фонтаны
fahn-<u>tah</u>-nee

fuentes
<u>fwehn</u>-tehs

Some parks have a zoo.   In the zoo there are . . .

elephants

éléphants
eh-leh-<u>fahng</u>

СЛОНЫ
slah-<u>nee</u>

elefantes
eh-leh-<u>fahn</u>-tehs

zebras

zēbres
zehb'r

зебры
z'yeh-bree

cebras
<u>theh</u>-brahs

hippopotamuses

hippopotames
ee-poh-poh-<u>tahm</u>

ГИППОПОТАМЫ
ghee-pah-pah-<u>tah</u>-mee

hipopótamos
ee-poh-<u>poh</u>-tah-mohs

penguins

pingouins
pehn-<u>gwehng</u>

ПИНГВИНЫ
peeng-<u>vee</u>-nee

pingüinos
pin-<u>gwee</u>-nohs

seals

phoques
fokk

ТЮЛЕНИ
t'you-l'<u>yeh</u>-nee

focas
<u>foh</u>-kahs

deer

cerfs
sehr

ОЛЕНИ
oh-l'<u>yeh</u>-nee

ciervos
s'<u>yehr</u>-vohs

foxes

bears

renards
ruh-<u>nahr</u>

ours
oorss

лисицы
lee-<u>see</u>-tsee

медведи
myed-v'<u>yeh</u>-dee

zorros
<u>thohr</u>-rohs

osos
<u>oh</u>-sohs

In every park
In New York

or Paris,

kites

cerfs-volants
sehr voh-lahng

воздушные змеи
vahz-doo'sh-nee-yeh z'meh-ee

cometas
koh-meh-tahs

balls

balles
bahl

мячи
m'yah-chee

pelotas
peh-loh-tahs

Moscow

or Madrid
Boys and girls,
Mothers and fathers
Have fun with . . .

swings

balançoires
bah-lawn-<u>swahr</u>

качели
kah-ch'yeh-lee

columpios
koh-<u>loom</u>-p'yohs

slides

toboggans
toh-boh-<u>gahng</u>

горки
<u>gohr</u>-kee

resbaladeros
rehs-bal-ah-<u>deh</u>-rohs

bicycles

bicyclettes
bee-see-<u>kleht</u>

велосипеды
v'yeh-lah-see-p'<u>yeh</u>-dee

bicicletas
bee-thee-<u>kleh</u>-tahs

jump ropes

cordes à sauter
kohrd ah soh-<u>teh</u>

скакалки
sk'ah-<u>kahl</u>-kee

combas
<u>kohm</u>-bahs

scooters

patinettes
pah-tee-<u>net</u>

самокаты
sah-mah-<u>kah</u>-tee

patinetes
pah-tee-<u>neh</u>-tehs

When boys and girls,
Mothers and fathers
get hungry in the park
In New York   or Paris,

Moscow
or Madrid
They eat . . .

soda

citronnade
see-troh-<u>nahd</u>

ситро
<u>see</u>-troh

limonada
lee-moh-<u>nah</u>-dah

candy

bonbon
bohng-bohng

конфеты
kohn-f'<u>yeh</u>-tee

bombón
bohm-<u>bohn</u>

pretzels	ice cream
bretzels	**glace**
bret-<u>sehl</u>	glahs
бублички	мороженое
<u>boob</u>-lee-chkee	mah-<u>roh</u>-zheh-nah-yeh
galletas	**helado**
gal-<u>yeh</u>-tahs	eh-<u>lah</u>-doh

When the day is gone
And everyone is tired

Fathers and mothers,
Sisters and brothers
Get ready to go home.

Everyone looks forward
To the next outing
In the park
In New York

or Paris,

Moscow

or Madrid.

Additional Words

boys	**garçons** gahr-sohng	мальчики mah'l-chee-kee	**muchachos** moo-chah-chohs
brother	**frère** frare	брат braht	**hermano** ehr-mah-noh
day	**jour** zhoor *zh* = the sound of *s* in pleasure	день d'yen	**día** dee-ah
father	**papa** pah-pah	папа pah-pah	**papá** pah-pah
fun	**amusement** ah-mewz-mahng	удовольствие oo-dah-vohl-stvee-yeh	**diversión** dee-vehr-see-ohn
girls	**filles** fee	девочки d'yeh-vah-ch'kee	**muchachas** moo-chah-chahs
good-by	**au revoir** ohr'vwahr	до свиданья doh svee-dah-n'yah	**adiós** ah-d'yoss
home	**maison** meh-zohng	домой dah-moy	**casa** kah-sah

English	French	Russian	Spanish
Madrid	**Madrid** mah-dreed	Мадрид mah-d'reed	**Madrid** mah-dreed
Moscow	**Moscou** mohs-koo	Москва mahs-k'vah	**Moscú** mohs-koo
mother	**maman** mah-mahng	мама mah-mah	**mamá** mah-mah
New York	**New York** new york	Нью Йорк new york	**Nueva York** nweh-vah york
outing	**excursion** ex-kewr-s'yohng	прогулка prah-gool-kah	**paseo** pah-seh-oh
Paris	**Paris** pah-ree	Париж pah-ree'zh	**París** pah-rees
park	**parc** pahrk	парк pahrk	**parque** pahr-keh
sister	**soeur** suhr	сестра s'yeh-strah	**hermana** ehr-mah-nah
visit	**visiter** vee-zee-teh	посещать pah-s'yeh-shchat'	**visitar** vee-see-tahr
zoo	**jardin zoologique** zhahr-dehng zoh-oh-loh-zheek	зоопарк zoh-oh-pahrk	**parque zoológico** pahr-keh thoh-oh-loh-hee-koh

Russian Alphabet

А а	ah as in arch	
Б б	b as in boy	
В в	v as in voice	
Г г	g as in good	
Д д	d as in do	
Е е	yeh as in yet	
Ё ё	yoh as in yoyo	
Ж ж	zh as in pleasure	
З з	z as in zero	
И и	ee as in feet	
Й й	y as in yeast	
К к	k as in keep	
Л л	l as in luck	
М м	m as in me	
Н н	n as in now	
О о	oh as in often when stressed, closer to ah when unstressed	

П п	p as in pie
Р р	r as in porridge
С с	s as in stay
Т т	t as in toy
У у	oo as in foot
Ф ф	f as in fix
Х х	kh as in hot
Ц ц	ts as in let's go
Ч ч	ch as in church
Ш ш	sh as in short
Щ щ	shch as in borshch
Ъ ъ	separation sign (')
Ы ы	ih as in a drawn-out is
Ь ь	soft sign (preceding consonant pronounced as if ee followed)
Э э	eh as in empty
Ю ю	yuh as you
Я я	yah as in yard